SAINSBURY'S

Quick and Easy Chicken

Carole Handslip

D1635593

Published exclusively for J Sainsbury plc
Stamford House Stamford Street
London SW1 9LL

by Martin Books
Simon & Schuster Consumer Group
Grafton House 64 Maids Causeway
Cambridge CB5 8DD

Published 1995

ISBN 0 85941 884 7

© 1995 Martin Books

Printed and bound in the UK by Bath Press Colourbooks
Design: Green Moore Lowenhoff
Photography: Hilary Moore
Styling: Marian Price
Food preparation: Cara Hobday
Typesetting: Spectrum Reprographics

Pictured on the front cover: Chicken and Mushroom Stroganoff (page 56)

Contents

Introduction

Although today's busy lifestyles leave us little time to spend in the kitchen fussing over complicated recipes, cooking need neither be dull nor predictable. One of the key secrets to quick-and-easy cooking is selecting your ingredients carefully. By choosing foods which require minimum preparation and are quick to cook, you can save time and still create delicious and original meals.

Chicken is, perhaps, the ultimate in 'fast food'. Not only is it one of the quickest meats to cook, but with the wide range of ready-prepared cuts and joints that are available, chicken is incredibly versatile too. Depending on whether you choose boneless breasts, thighs, wings or stir-fry strips, chicken can be grilled, casseroled, baked or fried. An even easier option is to buy the ready-cooked chicken found in the supermarkets' chilled cabinets. Roast chicken portions taste equally delicious in a cold salad or sandwich as they do eaten hot.

For a change of flavour, try corn-fed chickens – you'll recognise them from their bright yellow colour. Poussins, very young chickens, are another tasty option for a special occasion. They are very small birds, weighing between 500 and 750 g (1–1$\frac{1}{2}$ lb) each, and will usually be quite adequate for two people. As poussins are very tender they cook quickly – perfect for when you want to serve a whole bird without having leftovers.

You'll be surprised by just how many different ways there are to cook and serve chicken – these recipes run the gamut of flavours and ingredients. From favourite comfort foods such as Chicken and Vegetable Soup (page 10) to slightly more exotic recipes like Chicken and Mango Curry (page 64), to elegant dinner party dishes like Chicken and Mushroom Stroganoff (page 56), you're certain to find something to suit every mood, appetite or occasion. And best of all – they're simple and fast to prepare.

HOW TO PREPARE AND COOK CHICKEN SAFELY

I always keep a variety of chicken portions in my freezer for those days when I don't have time to get to the supermarket. However, although they are convenient to have on hand, you must take care when defrosting chicken. Whether defrosting a whole chicken or portions, pierce a hole in the wrappings and place the chicken on a plate to thaw. You can leave it to thaw in a cool place or overnight in the refrigerator. Make sure that it doesn't drip on any other foodstuffs when thawing, and cook it immediately once it is thawed. Never refreeze defrosted chicken.

Always use separate utensils for handling raw and cooked chicken as food-poisoning bacteria can be transferred from one to the other. Also ensure that work surfaces and chopping boards are cleaned and disinfected after preparing raw chicken. Wash your hands thoroughly after handling raw chicken.

It is essential that chicken is cooked until it is piping hot and any juices run clear. Pink or undercooked chicken can lead to a nasty bout of food poisoning. To test whether chicken is done, pierce the thickest part of the meat (the inside of the thigh is a good place for a whole roast bird). The juices should run clear with no trace of pink. If you are using cooked leftovers or previously cooked chicken in a recipe, make sure the chicken is kept cool in the fridge until it is needed.

RECIPE NOTES

All recipes in this book give ingredients in both metric (g, ml, etc.) and Imperial (oz, pints, etc.) measures. Use either set of quantities, but not a mixture of both, in any one recipe.

All teaspoons and tablespoons are level, unless otherwise stated.

1 teaspoon = a 5 ml spoon;

1 tablespoon = a 15 ml spoon.

Egg size is medium (size 3), unless otherwise stated.

Vegetables and fruit are medium-size unless otherwise stated.

Freshly ground black papper should be used throughout.

PREPARATION AND COOKING TIMES

Preparation and cooking times are included at the head of the recipes as a general guide; preparation times, especially, are approximate and timings are usually rounded to the nearest 5 minutes.

Preparation times include the time taken to prepare ingredients in the list, but not to make any 'basic' recipe.

The cooking times given at the heads of the recipes denote cooking periods when the dish can be left largely unattended, e.g. baking, and not the total amount of cooking for the recipe. Always read and follow the timings given for the steps of the recipe in the method.

Soups

Soups are one of my favourite meals. Quick and easy to make, they provide nourishing, easy-to-eat meals at any time of day.

Chicken stock is by far and away the best base for soup. It gives a delicious flavour and can be made into delicate consommés or hearty stews.

The better the stock the better the soup. Stock cubes are fine when you're short of time, but the real thing is far superior and, if made in advance, need be no more complicated to use than cubes. Next time you cook a chicken, save the carcase and any other unwanted bits. Put them in a saucepan with half an onion, a stick of celery and a carrot or leek. Top up with water, add a bay leaf, some parsley or a sprig of thyme, and bring to the boil. Simmer gently for 30–40 minutes and then strain into a bowl or jug. You can use it right away for any of the following soup recipes, or freeze it for use later.

Thai Noodle Soup

Preparation and cooking time: 8 minutes.
Freezing: not recommended. Serves 4.

This is a delicious soup, hot with fresh chilli, but with the fragrance of lemon grass and the texture of shiitake mushrooms. If shiitake mushrooms are not available, use oyster or chestnut mushrooms.

1 tablespoon groundnut oil
250 g (8 oz) stir-fry chicken strips
125 g (4 oz) shiitake mushrooms, sliced
   thinly
4 spring onions, sliced diagonally
½ red chilli, de-seeded and chopped finely

900 ml (1½ pints) chicken stock
1 stalk lemon grass, sliced thinly
50 g (2 oz) thin rice noodles, broken in pieces
1 tablespoon soy sauce, to serve
salt and freshly ground black pepper

❶ Heat the oil in a saucepan and stir-fry the chicken strips briskly for 1 minute to seal.

❷ Add the mushrooms, spring onions and chilli and stir-fry for 1 minute.

❸ Pour in the stock and add the lemon grass, noodles and seasoning to taste. Bring to a boil and simmer for 5 minutes until the noodles are softened.

❹ Stir in the soy sauce and transfer to a soup tureen to serve.

Spiced Potato and Chicken Soup

Preparation and cooking time: 30 minutes.
Freezing: not recommended. Serves 4.

This mildly spiced potato soup is flavoured with coconut and coriander, giving it a delicious taste and tantalising aroma.

2 tablespoons oil

250 g (8 oz) chicken breast, skinned and chopped roughly

1 onion, chopped

1 garlic clove, chopped

1 teaspoon turmeric

1 teaspoon cumin seeds

1 teaspoon ground coriander

750 g (1½ lb) potatoes, diced

750 ml (1½ pints) chicken stock

3 tablespoons coconut powder

4 tablespoons milk

1 tablespoon chopped fresh coriander

4 tablespoons yogurt, to serve

salt and freshly ground black pepper

❶ Heat the oil in a pan, fry the chicken to seal and then remove from the pan and set aside.

❷ Add the onion, garlic, spices and diced potatoes to the pan and fry, stirring constantly, for 1 minute.

❸ Stir in the stock, season to taste and bring to a boil. Cover and simmer gently for 15 minutes.

❹ Mix the coconut powder with the milk. Return the chicken to the pan with the chopped coriander and coconut paste and cook for 5 minutes more.

❺ Serve in bowls with a swirl of yogurt on each.

Chicken and Vegetable Soup

Preparation and cooking time: 35 minutes.
Freezing: recommended. Serves 4.

This is a homely and very filling soup. Served with crusty bread it makes a meal in itself.

2 chicken legs
1 large potato, diced
1 large carrot, diced
1 large leek, chopped
1 onion, chopped
2 celery sticks, chopped

1 turnip, chopped
bay leaf
900 ml (1½ pints) boiling water
2 tablespoons chopped fresh parsley
2 tablespoons double cream
salt and freshly ground black pepper

❶ Put the chicken legs in a large saucepan with the vegetables and bay leaf, and season to taste.

❷ Pour the boiling water over, bring back to a boil, cover and simmer gently for 20 minutes or until the chicken is cooked through.

❸ Remove the chicken from the pan with a slotted spoon. Cut off all the flesh, dice and return to the saucepan with the parsley and cream.

❹ Skim off any fat floating on the surface. Reheat and transfer to a soup tureen to serve.

Chicken, Carrot and Coriander Soup

Preparation and cooking time: 15 minutes.
Freezing: not recommended. Serves 4.

This delicious soup from Patagonian Chile is warming and nourishing. Use Basmati rice for its distinctive fragrance and flavour.

2 tablespoons sunflower oil
1 onion, chopped
2 garlic cloves, chopped
50 g (2 oz) Basmati rice
2 carrots, sliced thinly

900 ml (1½ pints) chicken stock
175 g (6 oz) cooked chicken breast, chopped
3 tablespoons chopped fresh coriander
salt and freshly ground black pepper

❶ Heat the oil in a pan and fry the onion until softened.

❷ Add the garlic and fry for 1 minute.

❸ Add the rice, carrots and stock, season to taste and bring to a boil.

❹ Cover and simmer for 10 minutes. Stir in the cooked chicken and coriander and heat through. Serve hot.

Chicken Soup Basquaise

Preparation and cooking time: 30 minutes.
Freezing: recommended. Serves 4.

This rich and filling tomato-based soup with chunks of chicken and chorizo sausage makes a hearty supper dish.

2 tablespoons olive oil
1 onion, chopped
125 g (4 oz) chicken breast, chopped
1 red pepper, de-seeded and chopped
1 garlic clove, chopped

400 g (13 oz) can of chopped tomatoes
600 ml (1 pint) chicken stock
50 g (2 oz) long-grain rice
125 g (4 oz) chorizo sausage, sliced
salt and freshly ground black pepper

❶ Heat the oil in a saucepan and add the onion, chicken, red pepper and garlic. Fry for 5 minutes, stirring occasionally.

❷ Add the tomatoes, stock and rice and bring to a boil. Cover and simmer gently for 15 minutes or until the rice is cooked.

❸ Add the chorizo sausage, season to taste and pour into a tureen. Serve with crusty bread.

Chicken and Watercress Soup

Preparation and cooking time: 12 minutes.
Freezing: not recommended. Serves 4.

This very quick soup is economical as well as easy. The sherry adds an extra warming element to its delicate flavour.

1.25 litres (2¼ pints) chicken stock
25 g (1 oz) vermicelli, broken in pieces
4 spring onions, sliced
125 g (4 oz) button mushrooms, sliced

1 bunch watercress, washed and chopped
75 g (3 oz) cooked chicken, chopped
2 tablespoons sherry
salt and freshly ground black pepper

❶ Put the stock in a saucepan and bring to a boil. Sprinkle in the vermicelli, stir to separate it and cook for 2 minutes.

❷ Add the spring onions, mushrooms and watercress and boil for 1–2 minutes, until the noodles are cooked.

❸ Add the chicken and sherry, season to taste and heat through.

Starters and Light Meals

Chicken is the ideal meat for a starter or light meal. Light, easily sliced and visually appealing, it can be served cold with a variety of salads. Quickly and easily deep-fried or sautéed, it can be used as the basis for an almost unlimited number of hot dishes.

One of my favourite starters is Smoked Chicken with Palm Hearts and Papaya (below). Served with a lime vinaigrette, it has a wonderfully refreshing and exotic taste. I discovered another exotic recipe on a recent trip to South America. Chicken Churrasco (page 16) is made by stuffing thin slices of chicken, avocado and tomato into hot bread – it's absolutely delicious but you'll need to have several paper napkins on hand to catch the juices!

Less exotic but very tasty – and inexpensive – chicken livers make an excellent quick snack or starter. Lightly fried with onion, garlic and a few herbs, they can be chopped up or made into a pâté and served with tomatoes, a chunk of fresh bread and a glass of red wine.

Smoked Chicken with Palm Hearts and Papaya

Preparation time: 15 minutes.
Freezing: not recommended. Serves 6.

Palm hearts are the tender shoots of palms. When fresh, they are cooked and served like asparagus. Delicious tinned in brine, they are a wonderful addition to this smoked chicken salad.

1 papaya, halved and de-seeded
175 g (6 oz) smoked chicken slices
400 g (13 oz) canned palm hearts, drained
2 tablespoons pine kernels, browned
1 tablespoon chopped fresh chervil, to garnish
melba toast, to serve

For the lime vinaigrette:
grated zest and juice of 1 lime
3 tablespoons olive oil
2 teaspoons clear honey
salt and freshly ground black pepper

❶ Peel the papaya and cut in slices lengthways. Arrange on 6 plates, alternating with slices of chicken.

❷ Slice the palm hearts and scatter them over the chicken with the pine kernels.

❸ Whisk together the dressing ingredients in a small bowl and drizzle over the salad.

❹ Garnish with the fresh chervil and serve with melba toast.

Chicken Churrasco

Preparation and cooking time: 15 minutes.
Freezing: not recommended. Serves 2–4.

This is a very popular snack in Chile and is really a sandwich of sorts. It can be made with either minute steak or thinly sliced chicken and is stuffed full with mashed avocado, tomatoes and mayonnaise. Although it's rather messy to eat, the taste is well worth it.

1 tablespoon olive oil

2 skinless, boneless chicken breasts, sliced

1 loaf ciabatta bread, warmed

3 tablespoons mayonnaise

1 avocado, halved and stoned

1 teaspoon lemon juice

2 tomatoes, sliced

salt and freshly ground black pepper

❶ Heat the oil in a pan and fry the chicken for 2–3 minutes, turning once until cooked through. Season well.

❷ Slice the loaf in half lengthways and spread the bottom half with some of the mayonnaise. Arrange the chicken on top.

❸ Scoop the flesh from the avocado and mash with the lemon juice. Season to taste and spread it on top of the chicken.

❹ Arrange the tomato slices on the avocado and spread the rest of the mayonnaise over the top.

❺ Top with the other half of the loaf and cut in 2–4 pieces to serve.

Chicken and Mango Vinaigrette

Preparation and cooking time: 15 minutes.
Freezing: not recommended. Serves 4.

This simple dish has a lovely combination of flavours which are enhanced by a lime-spiked mango dressing.

1 large mango
grated zest and juice of 1 lime
2 tablespoons olive oil
a few drops of tabasco sauce
1 tablespoon chopped coriander
4 tablespoons yogurt

175 g (6 oz) cooked chicken breast, sliced
1 head chicory, sliced diagonally
salt and freshly ground black pepper
fresh coriander sprigs or lime wedges, to
    garnish

❶ Slice the mango in half lengthways, cutting down both sides of the stone as closely as possible.

❷ Peel off the skin and discard. Cut one half of the mango in short slices and put in a bowl.

❸ Purée the remaining mango in a food processor with the lime zest and juice,

olive oil, tabasco and seasoning to taste. Blend until smooth, and then stir in the coriander and yogurt.

❹ Add the sliced chicken breast and chicory to the chopped mango, pour the dressing over and toss well.

❺ Serve on individual plates, garnished with lime wedges or coriander sprigs.

Chicken Goujons with Red Pepper Relish

Preparation and cooking time: 25 minutes.
Freezing: not recommended. Serves 4.

Deep-fry the goujons just before you eat so that they are crisp and hot.

250 g (8 oz) boneless chicken breast, cut in
   5 cm (2-inch) strips
1 egg, beaten
50 g (2 oz) fresh breadcrumbs
oil for deep frying
For the red pepper relish:
1 red pepper, skinned, de-seeded and chopped
1 shallot, chopped

1 garlic clove, crushed
1 tablespoon chopped fresh parsley
½ teaspoon caster sugar
2 teaspoons coarse-grained mustard
1 teaspoon cider vinegar
2 tablespoons mayonnaise
1 tablespoon capers, chopped
salt and freshly ground black pepper

❶ Mix together the ingredients for the relish.
❷ Dip the chicken in the egg a few times and roll in the breadcrumbs.
❸ Heat the oil to 180°C/350°F, or until a cube of bread turns golden brown in 30 seconds.
❹ Fry the chicken strips for 2–3 minutes until golden brown. Drain on kitchen paper and serve with the relish.

Puff Pastry Croûtes with Chicken and Roquefort

Preparation and cooking time: 25 minutes.
Freezing: recommended for filling only. Serves 4.

Quicker than a pie, but just as delicious!

125 g (4 oz) puff pastry slices, cut in 10 cm
   (4-inch) triangles
1 egg, beaten
2 tablespoons olive oil
500 g (1 lb) skinless, boneless chicken
   breast, cubed
1 large leek, chopped

1 garlic clove, chopped
1 tablespoon plain flour
175 ml (6 fl oz) chicken stock
25 g (1 oz) Roquefort cheese, crumbled
2 tablespoons double cream
1 tablespoon coarse-grained mustard
salt and freshly ground black pepper

❶ Preheat the oven to Gas Mark 7/ 230°C/425°F. Place the pastry triangles on a baking sheet and lightly score with a lattice pattern. Brush with egg and bake for 10–12 minutes.
❷ Heat the oil and fry the chicken until lightly browned. Remove from the pan.
❸ Add the leek and garlic and fry for 3 minutes. Return the chicken to the pan.
❹ Stir in the flour, gradually add the stock and bring to a boil, stirring until thickened. Cover and simmer for 10 minutes. Add the cheese, cream, mustard and seasoning, and heat gently.
❺ Serve on individual plates with a pastry croûte and broccoli.

Chicken Croissants

Preparation and cooking time: 15 minutes.
Freezing: not recommended. Serves 2–4.

This delicious quick snack has a creamy filling of chicken and bacon stuffed into a croissant and then heated in a very hot oven until crisp.

15 g (½ oz) butter

3 spring onions, chopped

2 rashers streaky bacon, chopped

15 g (½ oz) plain flour

175 ml (6 fl oz) milk

75 g (3 oz) cooked chicken, chopped

4 croissants

salt and freshly ground black pepper

❶ Preheat the oven to Gas Mark 8/ 230°C/450°F.
❷ Melt the butter in a saucepan, add the spring onions and bacon and cook for 3 minutes, or until turning brown.
❸ Remove from the heat, stir in the flour and gradually blend in the milk.
❹ Return to the heat and cook, stirring constantly, until thickened. Add the chicken and season to taste.
❺ Slice the croissants horizontally from the rounded side, leaving them hinged at the tips.
❻ Divide the filling between the croissants and press them well together. Arrange them on a baking sheet and bake for 4 minutes until crisp and hot.

Chicken Liver and Mushroom Pâté

Preparation and cooking time: 15 minutes.
Freezing: recommended. Serves 6.

The addition of mushrooms adds flavour and counters the richness of the chicken livers.

2 tablespoons olive oil

25 g (1 oz) butter

1 onion, chopped

250 g (8 oz) chicken livers

2 garlic cloves, chopped

125 g (4 oz) mushrooms, chopped roughly

1 teaspoon chopped fresh thyme

1 tablespoon chopped fresh parsley

2 tablespoons brandy

salt and freshly ground black pepper

❶ Heat the oil and butter in a frying pan and sauté the onion until softened.
❷ Add the chicken livers, garlic and mushrooms and stir-fry for 4 minutes, or until the livers are well cooked.
❸ Cool slightly and then transfer to a food processor or electric blender. Add the herbs and brandy, season to taste and purée until fairly smooth.
❹ Serve with thin triangles of toast.

Flageolet Beans with Chicken and Olives

Preparation and cooking time: 15 minutes.
Freezing: recommended. Serves 4.

This rich Mediterranean dish is given an extra lift with the addition of balsamic vinegar.

2 tablespoons olive oil

2 garlic cloves, chopped

250 g (8 oz) skinless chicken breast, chopped

4 courgettes, sliced thinly

400 g (13 oz) can of chopped tomatoes

2 × 420 g cans of flageolet beans, rinsed and drained

10 olives, halved and stoned

2 tablespoons chopped fresh parsley

2 teaspoons balsamic vinegar

1 teaspoon soft brown sugar

salt and freshly ground black pepper

❶ Heat the oil in a heavy-based pan. Add the garlic, chicken and courgettes and cook for 3–4 minutes, stirring.

❷ Add the tomatoes, beans and olives and cook for 2 minutes more.

❸ Add the parsley, vinegar and sugar, season to taste and mix together well. Serve hot or cold.

Chilli Chicken with Guacamole

Preparation and cooking time: 15 minutes.
Freezing: not recommended. Serves 4.

Spicy chicken strips go beautifully with the soft texture of guacamole.

2 tablespoons oil

2 teaspoons paprika

½ teaspoon chilli powder

250 g (8 oz) skinless, boneless chicken breast, cut in strips

1 head chicory, with leaves separated

For the guacamole:

1 large avocado

1 tablespoon lemon juice

2 tomatoes, skinned and chopped

1 garlic clove, crushed

2 spring onions, chopped finely

¼ teaspoon tabasco sauce

1 tablespoon chopped fresh coriander

salt and freshly ground black pepper

❶ Combine the oil, paprika and chilli powder in a bowl and marinate the chicken.

❷ Meanwhile, make the guacamole. Halve the avocado, remove the stone and scoop the flesh into a bowl. Add the lemon juice and mash with a fork.

❸ Add the remaining ingredients, season to taste and mix thoroughly.

❹ Heat a heavy-based frying pan, add the chicken and marinade and cook for 3–4 minutes, turning constantly until the chicken is cooked through.

❺ Arrange the chicory leaves on 4 plates and top with the guacamole and chicken.

Everyday Meals

Chicken is such a versatile food: ideal for marinating, it can be spiced, devilled or curried; stir-fried, deep-fried or sautéed; stewed, roasted or grilled; boiled or barbecued. And it's always good to eat.

Chicken is a very useful standby for too-busy-to-cook cooks as the supermarket does all the jointing. Pies and bakes are but a moment's work, and you need no longer eat ten chickens in order to barbecue a few drumsticks. I always keep a supply of chicken breasts in the deep freeze, ready for quick thawing and transformation into anything from a stir-fry to a kebab.

Chicken and Leek au Gratin

Preparation time: 15 minutes + 15 minutes baking.
Freezing: not recommended. Serves 4.

This is a particularly useful dish at Christmas time when you have plenty of leftover chicken and ham.

25 g (1 oz) butter

1 tablespoon sunflower oil

500 g (1 lb) leeks, sliced

1 garlic clove, crushed

4 teaspoons flour

300 g (½ pint) milk

300 g (10 oz) cooked chicken, cut in chunks

125 g (4 oz) cooked ham, cut in cubes

2 tablespoons chopped fresh parsley

1 tablespoon coarse-grained mustard

25 g (1 oz) fresh breadcrumbs

50 g (2 oz) Cheddar cheese, grated

salt and freshly ground black pepper

❶ Preheat the oven to Gas Mark 5/190°C/375°F.

❷ Melt the butter and oil in a heavy-based pan and fry the leeks and garlic for 10 minutes, stirring occasionally.

❸ Stir in the flour, and then gradually add the milk and cook, stirring until thickened.

❹ Remove from the heat and stir in the chicken, ham, parsley and mustard, and season to taste. Turn into a shallow 1.2-litre (2-pint) ovenproof dish.

❺ Mix together the breadcrumbs and cheese and sprinkle over the top. Bake for 15 minutes until golden brown. Serve with a green salad.

Chicken, Bacon and Mushroom Pie

Preparation and cooking time: 25 minutes.
Freezing: recommended (before cooking). Serves 4.

This quick, easy and very tasty pie is made with filo pastry which makes a very effective decorative topping when scrunched up into folds.

2 tablespoons olive oil

350 g (12 oz) boneless chicken breast, cut in strips

125 g (4 oz) rindless bacon, chopped

350 g (12 oz) mushrooms, sliced

2 garlic cloves, chopped

4 spring onions, sliced

2 tablespoons flour

250 ml (8 fl oz) chicken stock

4 tablespoons double cream

3–5 sheets filo pastry

15 g (½ oz) melted butter

1 teaspoon sesame seeds

salt and freshly ground black pepper

❶ Preheat the oven to Gas Mark 5/190°C/375°F.

❷ Heat the oil in a pan, add the chicken and bacon and fry quickly for 3–4 minutes, stirring constantly.

❸ Add the mushrooms, garlic and spring onions and fry for 2 minutes more. Stir in the flour.

❹ Remove from the heat and blend in the stock. Bring to a boil and cook, stirring until thickened.

❺ Add the cream, season to taste and turn into a 900 ml (1½-pint) oblong ovenproof dish.

❻ Lay a sheet of filo pastry on a flat surface and brush it with butter. Scrunch it up with your fingers and arrange it on one end of the dish. Repeat with additional sheets until the pie's surface is covered. Sprinkle with sesame seeds and cook in the oven for 15 minutes until golden brown.

Chicken Stir-fry with Yellow Bean Sauce

Preparation and cooking time: 15 minutes.
Freezing: not recommended. Serves 4.

A stir-fry is a very adaptable recipe as you can vary the vegetables depending on what you have on hand. Just remember to cut the vegetables to a similar size and choose a colourful mixture when possible.

3 tablespoons groundnut oil

50 g (2 oz) cashew nuts

350 g (12 oz) stir-fry chicken strips

1 garlic clove, chopped

1 bunch spring onions, cut in 2.5 cm (1-inch) lengths

1 red pepper, de-seeded and cut in strips

3 courgettes, cut in matchsticks

150 g (5 oz) yellow bean sauce

2 tablespoons dry sherry

❶ Heat 2 tablespoons of the oil in a wok and stir-fry the cashew nuts until they begin to brown. Remove from the pan.

❷ Add the chicken and stir-fry briskly for 2–5 minutes until sealed all over. Remove from the pan.

❸ Add the remaining oil to the wok, stir in the garlic, spring onions, red pepper and courgettes and stir-fry for 2 minutes.

❹ Return the chicken and cashew nuts to the pan with the yellow bean sauce and the sherry. Heat through and serve with egg noodles.

Chicken Chow Mein

Preparation and cooking time: 15 minutes.
Freezing: not recommended. Serves 4.

Chow mein can be made with any vegetables you have available. Use oyster or button mushrooms if you can't find shiitake mushrooms.

250 g (8 oz) thread egg noodles

2 tablespoons groundnut oil

350 g (12 oz) chicken breast, cut in strips

1 onion, sliced

2 garlic cloves, chopped

2.5 cm (1-inch) piece of fresh root ginger, chopped

1 red pepper, de-seeded and sliced thinly

125 g (4 oz) shiitake mushrooms, sliced

2 tablespoons sherry

1 teaspoon cornflour

250 g (8 oz) baby spinach leaves

2 tablespoons soy sauce

1 teaspoon sesame oil

❶ Put the noodles in a saucepan, pour boiling water over, bring to a boil and simmer for 3 minutes. Drain thoroughly.

❷ Heat the oil in a wok, add the chicken and onion and stir-fry for 2 minutes, until the chicken is sealed all over.

❸ Add the garlic, ginger, red pepper and mushrooms and stir-fry for 2 minutes.

❹ Blend the sherry and cornflour and add to the wok with the spinach and soy sauce. Stir-fry to wilt the spinach.

❺ Add the drained noodles and sesame oil to the wok. Stir well to mix and serve.

Chicken Chilli

Preparation and cooking time: 30 minutes.
Freezing: recommended. Serves 4.

This hot and spicy chicken chilli is served topped with yogurt and avocado and then lavishly sprinkled with coriander – a magical combination. Serve with plain boiled rice.

2 tablespoons sunflower oil

1 onion, chopped

2 celery sticks, chopped

500 g (1 lb) minced chicken

2 garlic cloves, chopped

¼ teaspoon chilli powder

1 teaspoon ground coriander

400 g (13 oz) can of chopped tomatoes

120 ml (4 fl oz) chicken stock

2 tablespoons tomato purée

2 × 420 g cans of red kidney beans, rinsed and drained

salt and freshly ground black pepper

To serve:

1 large avocado, halved and stoned

150 g (5 oz) yogurt

2 tablespoons chopped fresh coriander

❶ Heat the oil in a heavy-based pan and fry the onion and celery for 5 minutes until softened.

❷ Add the chicken and garlic and fry quickly, stirring constantly, until sealed all over.

❸ Add the spices and cook for 1 minute more, and then add the tomatoes, stock, tomato purée and seasoning to taste.

Bring to a boil, cover and simmer for 15 minutes.

❹ Add the kidney beans and simmer for 5 minutes.

❺ Just before serving the chilli, peel and slice the avocado. Spoon yogurt over each serving, top with avocado slices, sprinkle generously with coriander and serve with boiled rice.

Chicken and Pasta Bake

Preparation and cooking time: 25 minutes.
Freezing: not recommended. Serves 4.

Use your favourite cheese in this creamy gratin dish.

2 tablespoons olive oil
1 onion, chopped
500 g (1 lb) chicken mince
2 garlic cloves, chopped
¼ teaspoon cinnamon
1 tablespoon paprika
1 tablespoon flour

250 g (8 oz) courgettes, sliced thinly
150 ml (¼ pint) tomato juice
400 g (13 oz) can of chopped tomatoes
1 tablespoon chopped fresh oregano
250 g (8 oz) pasta shapes
125 g (4 oz) Gruyère cheese, grated
salt and freshly ground black pepper

❶ Heat the oil in a frying pan and fry the onion until softened. Add the mince and garlic and stir-fry, for about 3 minutes.

❷ Add the cinnamon, paprika, flour, courgettes, tomato juice, tomatoes, oregano and seasoning to taste. Bring to a boil, cover and cook for 10 minutes.

❸ Meanwhile, cook the pasta in a large pan of salted boiling water for 5 minutes. Drain and mix with the mince sauce. Preheat the grill.

❹ Transfer to a gratin dish and top with the cheese. Place under a grill for 2–3 minutes, until brown and bubbling.

Chicken Liver and Tomatoes with Fettucini

Preparation and cooking time: 20 minutes.
Freezing: recommended. Serves 4.

This economical meal is made even quicker if you use fresh pasta.

4 tablespoons olive oil
375 g (12 oz) chicken livers
2 onions, chopped
2 garlic cloves, chopped
250 g (8 oz) mushrooms, sliced
4 tomatoes, skinned and chopped

1 tablespoon flour
1 tablespoon chopped fresh marjoram
2 tablespoons medium-dry sherry
4 tablespoons tomato juice
500 g (1 lb) fresh fettucini
salt and freshly ground black pepper

❶ Heat the oil in a pan and fry the chicken livers for 4 minutes until they are browned. Remove from the pan and chop, reserving the juices.

❷ Add the onions and cook until softened. Then add the garlic, mushrooms and tomatoes and stir-fry for 2 minutes.

❸ Stir in the flour, marjoram, sherry, tomato juice, seasoning and the chopped livers. Bring to a boil and simmer for 2 minutes.

❹ Meanwhile, cook the fettucini as per pack instructions and drain thoroughly. Mix with the sauce and serve with a green salad.

Chicken Thighs in Mustard Sauce

Preparation and cooking time: 30 minutes.
Freezing: not recommended. Serves 4.

The exact cooking time for this tangy dish will depend on the size of the chicken thighs. If you are short of time you can make this recipe using strips of chicken breast which will need only 3 minutes simmering.

2 tablespoons olive oil

4 large or 8 small skinless chicken thighs
(weighing about 500 g/1 lb total)

2 garlic cloves, chopped

1 dessert apple, cored, quartered and sliced

150 ml (¼ pint) white wine

2 teaspoons cornflour

4 tablespoons milk

2 tablespoons coarse-grained mustard

4 tablespoons double cream

salt and freshly ground black pepper

❶ Heat the oil in a heavy-based pan and fry the chicken thighs on both sides until browned.

❷ Add the garlic and apple and fry for 1 minute more, stirring occasionally.

❸ Pour the wine over, cover and simmer for 20 minutes.

❹ Blend the cornflour with the milk and add it to the pan with the mustard, cream and seasoning to taste.

❺ Bring to a boil and simmer for a few minutes until thickened. Serve with plain boiled Basmati rice and a green salad.

Chicken and Mushroom Risotto

Preparation and cooking time: 30 minutes.
Freezing: not recommended. Serves 4.

Choose a variety of mushrooms to give this recipe a more interesting flavour and texture. Black trumpet, chanterelle and oyster mushrooms make a really colourful and fragrant risotto.

2 tablespoons olive oil

350 g (12 oz) skinless chicken breast, chopped

1 onion, chopped

2 garlic cloves, chopped

125 g (4 oz) smoked bacon, chopped

1 red pepper, de-seeded and chopped

175 g (6 oz) Carnaroli or Arborio rice

1 tablespoon tomato purée

600 ml (1 pint) hot chicken stock

25 g (1 oz) butter

350 g (12 oz) mixed mushrooms, sliced or halved

2 tablespoons chopped fresh parsley

50 g (2 oz) parmesan shavings, to serve

salt and freshly ground black pepper

❶ Heat the oil in a heavy-based pan and stir-fry the chicken until sealed all over. Remove from the pan.

❷ Add the onion, garlic, bacon and red pepper and fry for 5 minutes, stirring occasionally.

❸ Stir in the rice, tomato purée, stock, and seasoning to taste.

❹ Return the chicken to the pan and cover. Simmer gently for 15 minutes until the stock is absorbed, adding a little extra liquid towards the end if necessary.

❺ Meanwhile, heat the butter in a frying pan and fry the mushrooms for 5 minutes, stirring occasionally.

❻ Stir the mushrooms and their juices and the parsley into the risotto and transfer to a serving dish. Sprinkle with parmesan and serve with a crisp green salad.

Warm Lentil and Spiced Chicken Salad

Preparation time: 20 minutes.
Freezing: not recommended. Serves 4.

This very quick salad uses canned lentils. If you prefer to cook your own, use green lentils as they stay whole when cooked and look much more attractive in a salad.

2 tablespoons oil
350 g (12 oz) chicken breast, sliced
125 g (4 oz) smoked bacon, cut in strips
2 garlic cloves, chopped
1 tablespoon ground coriander
¼ teaspoon chilli powder
6 spring onions, sliced

4 tomatoes, skinned and cut in strips
2 × 220 g cans of lentils, drained
salad leaves, to garnish
For the dressing:
2 tablespoons olive oil
2 teaspoons wine vinegar
2 teaspoons soy sauce

❶ Heat the oil in a heavy-based pan and fry the chicken and bacon for 3–4 minutes until the chicken is sealed all over.

❷ Add the garlic, coriander, chilli powder and spring onions and fry for 1 minute more.

❸ Add the tomatoes and drained lentils and heat through.

❹ Meanwhile, mix all the dressing ingredients together, pour over the lentil mixture and stir until well coated. Turn into a shallow serving dish and garnish with salad leaves.

Peulla Salad

Preparation and cooking time: 20 minutes.
Freezing: not recommended. Serves 4.

Avocado, tomato and coriander are natural partners and are served together in many ways in Chile. Serve this salad with crusty bread to mop up the juices.

4 tablespoons olive oil

2 tablespoons lime juice

½ red chilli, de-seeded and chopped finely

½ teaspoon caster sugar

3 tablespoons chopped fresh coriander

½ teaspoon salt

2 avocados, halved and stoned

1 onion, sliced

350 g (12 oz) cooked chicken breast, chopped

1 small red pepper, de-seeded and chopped

12 cherry tomatoes, halved

½ Iceberg lettuce, shredded

❶ Mix the oil, lime juice, chopped chilli, sugar, coriander and salt in a screw-topped jar and shake vigorously.

❷ Cut the avocados in chunks and place in a large bowl with the onion. Pour the dressing over them, mix well and leave for 5 minutes.

❸ Stir in the chicken, red pepper and tomatoes. Toss together thoroughly and serve on a bed of shredded lettuce.

Chicken Liver Salad with Hot Tomato Dressing

Preparation and cooking time: 20 minutes.
Freezing: not recommended. Serves 4.

Warm sautéed chicken livers served over crisp salad leaves with a hot tomato dressing and crunchy croûtons make an ideal lunch on a hot sunny day.

1 head frisée lettuce

a few radicchio leaves

2 heads red chicory, sliced diagonally

a few rocket leaves

6 tablespoons olive oil

4 slices French bread, cut in cubes

2 garlic cloves, chopped roughly

125 g (4 oz) thick bacon slices, chopped

350 g (12 oz) chicken livers

4 tomatoes, skinned and chopped roughly

1 tablespoon balsamic vinegar

1 tablespoon coarse-grained mustard

❶ Tear the frisée and radicchio leaves into bite-sized pieces and toss them in a salad bowl with the chicory and rocket.

❷ Heat 2 tablespoons of the olive oil in a frying pan and fry the bread cubes until golden. Remove from the pan, drain on kitchen paper and keep warm.

❸ Add another 2 tablespoons of the oil to the pan and fry the garlic, bacon and chicken livers for 5 minutes, stirring occasionally, until tender. Remove from

the pan, slice the livers roughly and keep warm.

❹ Add the remaining oil to the pan with the tomatoes, balsamic vinegar and mustard and stir to dissolve any juices. Cook long enough to heat the tomatoes through. Pour over the salad leaves, spoon the livers and bacon on top and sprinkle with the croûtons. Serve immediately.

Weekend Specials

The weekend is the time to be adventurous and cook something special. These dishes take a little time to prepare, but by using a few well-chosen ingredients and by taking care with the presentation, you can create an elegant main course to impress your friends.

For these recipes, time is saved by making use of prepared cuts such as prime breast fillet and stir-fry strips. Poussins, very young chickens, are also a good choice – they look more attractive than joints and you can serve them 'spatchcocked' or split in half.

Quick Coq au Vin

Preparation and cooking time: 15 minutes.
Freezing: recommended. Serves 4.

Chicken strips, bacon and mushrooms are cooked in a red wine and garlic sauce in a very quick adaptation of the traditional recipe.

2 tablespoons olive oil

1 onion, sliced

350 g (12 oz) stir-fry chicken strips

175 g (6 oz) bacon steaks, cut in thick strips

175 g (6 oz) button mushrooms

2 garlic cloves, chopped

1 tablespoon flour

1 teaspoon soft brown sugar

1 tablespoon tomato purée

150 ml (¼ pint) red wine

50 ml (2 fl oz) chicken stock

1 bay leaf

1 tablespoon chopped fresh parsley, to garnish

salt and freshly ground black pepper

❶ Heat the oil in a heavy-based pan, add the onion and fry until softened.

❷ Add the chicken, bacon, mushrooms and garlic and fry briskly for 4 minutes, stirring constantly.

❸ Stir in the flour, sugar and tomato purée, and then pour in the wine and stock with seasoning to taste. Bring to a boil, add the bay leaf and simmer gently for 5 minutes.

❹ Remove the bay leaf, turn on to a serving dish, sprinkle with the parsley and serve with new potatoes and vegetables.

Chicken Parmigiana

Preparation and cooking time: 35 minutes.
Freezing: not recommended. Serves 4.

Aubergine is the perfect partner for tomatoes and together they make a tasty topping for chicken.

4 × 175 g (6 oz) skinless chicken breasts

2 tablespoons olive oil

1 large aubergine, sliced lengthways

2 garlic cloves, chopped

400 g (13 oz) can of chopped tomatoes

1 teaspoon sugar

2 teaspoons chopped fresh oregano

250 g (8 oz) mozzarella, sliced

2 tablespoons grated parmesan cheese

salt and freshly ground black pepper

❶ Preheat the oven to Gas Mark 6/ 200°C/400°F.

❷ Sprinkle salt and pepper all over the chicken breasts. Heat the oil in a pan and fry them for about 4 minutes, turning once. Remove from the pan.

❸ Fry the aubergine slices for 1 minute on each side, and then add the garlic, tomatoes, sugar, oregano and seasoning to taste. Cover and cook for 5 minutes.

❹ Lay the chicken in a shallow ovenproof dish, arrange the aubergine slices over the top and spoon the rest of the tomato sauce over.

❺ Lay the mozzarella over the chicken and sprinkle with the parmesan.

❻ Bake for 20 minutes until the cheese has melted and is just turning brown.

Warm Mushroom and Chicken on Salad Leaves

Preparation and cooking time: 10 minutes.
Freezing: not recommended. Serves 4.

This is a very quick, warm salad that can be made with any mixture of mushrooms. Chestnut mushrooms have a good firm texture and shiitake mushrooms have a meaty flavour. Try oyster mushrooms too.

a selection of salad leaves

2 tablespoons olive oil

300 g (10 oz) chicken breast, cut in strips

75 g (3 oz) back bacon, chopped roughly

2 garlic cloves, chopped

250 g (8 oz) mixed mushrooms

3 tablespoons sherry

1 tablespoon balsamic vinegar

salt and freshly ground black pepper

❶ Arrange a selection of salad leaves on 4 individual plates.

❷ Heat the oil in a frying pan and stir-fry the chicken and bacon for 1 minute until it is sealed all over.

❸ Add the garlic and mushrooms and stir-fry for 2 minutes more.

❹ Add the sherry, balsamic vinegar and seasoning and stir well to mix.

❺ Spoon the chicken mixture and its juices over the salad leaves and serve.

Spatchcocked Poussins

Preparation and cooking time: 30 minutes.
Freezing: recommended for rice and poussins before cooking.
Serves 4.

Spatchcocked birds have been cut open and flattened which means they cook faster. They need to be supported or held open with skewers. You can use other cuts of chicken for this recipe – breasts, legs, wings or halved poussins will work equally well. These are excellent when cooked on a barbecue.

4 × 425 g (14 oz) poussins

4 garlic cloves

2 tablespoons clear honey

2 tablespoons coarse-grained mustard

2 teaspoons ground coriander

¼ teaspoon chilli powder

1 tablespoon soy sauce

2 tablespoons sunflower oil

6 spring onions, chopped

½ teaspoon ground turmeric

750 g (1½ lb) cooked rice

2 tablespoons chopped fresh coriander

lemon wedges, to garnish

❶ Using poultry shears or a sharp knife, cut along both sides of each backbone and discard them. Place the poussins, breast up on a flat surface and press firmly on the head end to flatten them. Run a long bamboo skewer through the base of each leg to the wing diagonally opposite to keep them in place.

❷ Preheat the grill to medium. Crush 2 cloves of garlic and mix with the honey, mustard, coriander, chilli powder and soy sauce.

❸ Brush the poussins with the sauce and grill for 7 minutes on each side, or until cooked through, basting occasionally with more sauce.

❹ Meanwhile, heat the oil in a pan, chop the remaining garlic and fry it with the spring onions and turmeric for 1 minute. Add the cooked rice to the pan and mix thoroughly to give the rice an even colour. Add 1 tablespoon of the honey sauce along with the fresh coriander. Heat through for a couple of minutes.

❺ Serve the poussins with the rice, garnished with lemon wedges and accompanied by a crisp green salad.

Poussins with Garlic and Cider Vinegar

Preparation and cooking time: 40 minutes.
Freezing: recommended. Serves 4.

Poussins vary in size from 350 g (12 oz) to 650 g (1¼ lb) – the smaller ones being ideal for single servings. Although these young birds are very tender, they have not developed much flavour, so this is the perfect sauce for them – garlic, mustard and vinegar, mellowed with the addition of cream and sweetened with apples.

2 × 625 g (1¼ lb) poussins
25 g (1 oz) butter
1 tablespoon sunflower oil
2 dessert apples, peeled, cored and sliced
3 garlic cloves, chopped

4 tablespoons cider vinegar
2 tablespoons apple juice
1 tablespoon coarse-grained mustard
142 ml (5 fl oz) double cream
sprigs of watercress, to garnish (optional)

❶ Halve the poussins by cutting through the breasts with a sharp knife and then cutting down each side of the backbone and discarding the bone.

❷ Heat the butter and oil in a heavy-based pan and fry the apple slices on both sides until golden brown. Remove from the pan.

❸ Fry the poussins for 5 minutes on each side, until golden brown.

❹ Add the garlic, vinegar and apple juice. Cover and simmer gently for 15 minutes, until cooked through.

❺ Remove the poussins and keep warm. Add the mustard, cream and fried apples to the pan and heat through.

❻ Arrange the poussins on warm plates and spoon the sauce over them. Garnish with sprigs of watercress, if you like, and serve with new potatoes.

Parma Ham and Chicken Roulades

Preparation and cooking time: 40 minutes.
Freezing: not recommended. Serves 4.

This very attractive dish is full of interesting flavours. Parma ham encases succulent chicken, stuffed with blue cheese. A creamy wine sauce completes this elegant dinner party dish.

4 skinless chicken breasts
125 g (4 oz) Dolcelatte cheese, cut in 4 slices
4 large slices of Parma ham
2 sage leaves, cut in half
150 ml (¼ pint) white wine

25 g (1 oz) butter
1 tablespoon flour
6 tablespoons single cream
salt and freshly ground black pepper
sage leaves, to garnish

❶ Preheat the oven to Gas Mark 5/ 190°C/375°F.

❷ Using a sharp knife, cut a deep pocket in the thickest part of each chicken breast.

❸ Push a slice of cheese into each of the pockets.

❹ Wrap a slice of ham around each chicken breast and place them in a shallow ovenproof dish. Sprinkle with salt and pepper and top with the sage leaves. Pour in the wine and bake in the oven for 25 minutes until the chicken is cooked through.

❺ Pour off the juices into a jug, cover the chicken and keep warm.

❻ Heat the butter in a saucepan, stir in the flour and then blend in the juices. Bring to a boil and cook for 2 minutes. Add the cream and season to taste.

❼ Slice the chicken, arrange on individual serving plates, spoon a little sauce over the top and garnish with sage leaves.

Chicken and Mushroom Stroganoff

Preparation and cooking time: 20 minutes.
Freezing: not recommended. Serves 4.

Use a variety of wild mushrooms such as bright yellow chanterelle, black trumpet and oyster mushrooms. Sometimes you may be lucky enough to find *pied de mouton* or hedgehog mushrooms. If these are not in season, of course you can always use button or chestnut mushrooms.

2 tablespoons sunflower oil

350 g (12 oz) chicken fillet, cut in thin strips

1 large onion, sliced

25 g (1 oz) butter

2 garlic cloves, chopped

250 g (8 oz) wild mushrooms, sliced

2 tablespoons brandy

2 teaspoons Dijon mustard

142 ml (5 fl oz) double cream

salt and freshly ground black pepper

❶ Heat the oil in a frying pan and stir-fry the chicken for 2–3 minutes. Remove from the pan and set aside.

❷ Add the onion and fry gently until softened.

❸ Add the butter to the pan, heat until melted, and then add the garlic and mushrooms. Fry briskly for 2 minutes, stirring constantly.

❹ Return the chicken and its juices to the pan with the brandy, mustard and seasoning and mix together.

❺ Stir in the cream, bring to a boil and simmer for 2 minutes. Serve with Basmati rice and a green salad.

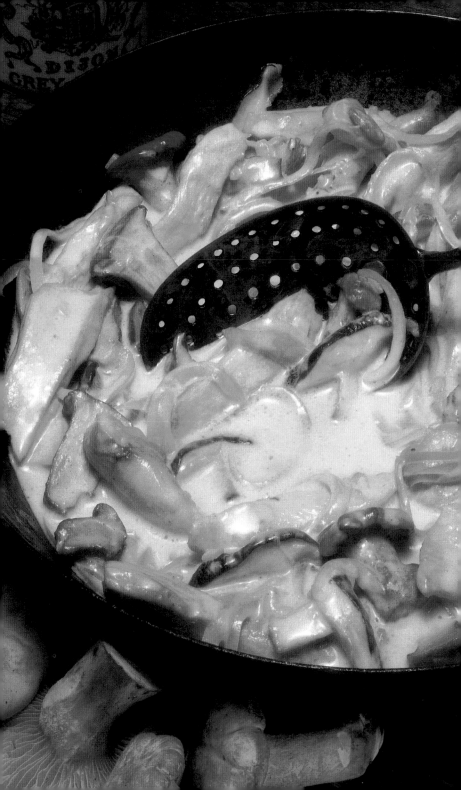

Chicken with Fennel and Coriander

Preparation and cooking time: 45 minutes.
Freezing: not recommended. Serves 4.

This dish has a simple but exciting combination of flavours. It looks quite stunning when piled on a large platter. Serve with a bowl of new potatoes.

2 tablespoons olive oil

4 chicken joints

250 g (8 oz) pickling onions, peeled

3 carrots, cut in sticks

1 head fennel, cut in wedges

2 garlic cloves, sliced

¼ teaspoon chilli powder

1 tablespoon ground coriander

300 ml (½ pint) white wine

400 g (13 oz) can of chopped tomatoes

350 g (12 oz) courgettes, cut in fingers

3 tablespoons chopped fresh coriander, to garnish

salt and freshly ground black pepper

❶ Heat the oil in a large flameproof casserole and fry the chicken joints, turning occasionally, until golden brown all over. Remove from the pan.

❷ Add the onions, carrots, fennel and garlic and fry, stirring, for 5 minutes.

❸ Stir in the chilli powder and coriander and fry for 1 minute. Add the wine and tomatoes with seasoning to taste and bring to a boil.

❹ Return the chicken to the pan and place the courgettes on top so that they cook in the steam. Cover and simmer for 30 minutes until the chicken is tender.

❺ Remove the chicken and vegetables and arrange them on a large platter. Cover and keep warm. Boil the liquor in the pan to reduce and strengthen the flavour and then spoon it over the chicken and sprinkle liberally with fresh coriander.

Filo Chicken Parcels

**Preparation and cooking time: 40 minutes.
Freezing: not recommended. Serves 4.**

These pretty filo pastry parcels are served with creamed leeks.

75 g (3 oz) butter

500 g (1 lb) prepared leeks, sliced thinly

2 tablespoons chopped fresh chives

1 teaspoon coarse-grained mustard

2 tablespoons double cream

1 tablespoon olive oil

300 g (10 oz) small prime breast fillet

8 sheets filo pastry, cut in 18 cm (7-inch)
　squares

50 g (2 oz) wafer-thin smoked ham

125 g (4 oz) Brie, cut in slices

salt and freshly ground black pepper

❶ Preheat the oven to Gas Mark 5/
190°C/375°F.

❷ Melt 25 g (1 oz) of the butter in a
heavy-based pan, add the leeks, season
and cover and cook for 15 minutes. Stir
in the chives, mustard and cream.

❸ Meanwhile, heat the oil in a pan and
brown the chicken for 5 minutes.

❹ Melt the remaining butter. Brush 1
filo square with butter, lay another on top
and arrange 2 chicken pieces in the
middle. Season well. Cover with a piece of
ham and then a piece of Brie.

❺ Fold the the pastry over to cover and
brush a third square with butter. Scrunch
it in folds and lay it on top of the parcel.

❻ Make 4 parcels, lay them on a baking
sheet and bake for 15 minutes until
golden. Serve with the creamed leeks.

Chicken with Asparagus and Tarragon

**Preparation and cooking time: 20 minutes.
Freezing: not recommended. Serves 4.**

This is an impressive looking dish with a delicate flavour.

250 g (8 oz) asparagus spears

2 tablespoons sunflower oil

1 onion, sliced thinly

350 g (12 oz) small prime chicken breast
　fillet

1 tablespoon flour

125 ml (4 fl oz) white wine

1 tablespoon chopped fresh tarragon

6 tablespoons double cream

salt and freshly ground black pepper

❶ Cut the asparagus in 5 cm (2-inch)
lengths, keeping the tips separate. Cook
the stalks in boiling salted water for 4
minutes, and then add the tips and cook
for 3 minutes. Drain and reserve 120 ml
(4 fl oz) of the liquid.

❷ Heat the oil and fry the onion and
chicken breasts until the meat is sealed.

❸ Remove from the heat and stir in the
flour. Gradually pour in the wine and the
asparagus liquid.

❹ Bring to a boil, stirring constantly.
Add the tarragon, season to taste, cover
and simmer for 3 minutes.

❺ Add the asparagus and cream and
heat through. Serve with new potatoes.

Faraway Flavours

Foods and dishes that would have seemed exotic and strange just a few years ago are now staples in our diets. From teryaki to tagine, biryani to bolognaise – we can pick these up from the local takeaway or just as easily buy the ingredients and make them ourselves. There are few countries in which chicken is not a staple food, and for this reason you'll find countless recipes whose origins are from faraway. However, these are not difficult to make at home and it can be great fun to recreate faraway flavours in your own kitchen.

Chicken Cazuela

Preparation and cooking time: 40 minutes.
Freezing: not recommended. Serves 4.

I discovered this hearty stew on a recent trip to Chile. Serve it with plenty of crusty bread for a filling and wholesome meal.

2 tablespoons sunflower oil
4 chicken legs, cut in half
2 onions, sliced
2 garlic cloves, chopped
2 carrots, cut in sticks
750 g (1½ lb) potatoes, cut in chunks
1 red pepper, de-seeded and chopped roughly
600 ml (1 pint) chicken stock
125 g (4 oz) peas
125 g (4 oz) green beans, topped and tailed
3 tablespoons chopped fresh coriander
salt and freshly ground black pepper

❶ Heat the oil in a heavy-based pan and fry the chicken legs until browned. Remove from the pan.

❷ Add the onions and garlic and fry for 5 minutes until softened.

❸ Stir in the carrots, potatoes, red pepper, stock and seasoning to taste. Bring to a boil, return the chicken to the pan, cover and simmer for 15 minutes.

❹ Add the peas and green beans and cook for 15 minutes more.

❺ Stir in the coriander and serve with crusty bread.

Chicken and Mango Curry

Preparation and cooking time: 25 minutes.
Freezing: recommended. Serves 4.

A mildly spiced, creamy curry flavoured with coconut cream and fresh coriander – this dish is sure to become a favourite.

2 tablespoons sunflower oil

500 g (1 lb) chicken breast, cut in cubes

1 onion, chopped

2 garlic cloves, chopped

1 teaspoon ground coriander

1 teaspoon cumin seeds

1 teaspoon turmeric

1 teaspoon ground ginger

25 g (1 oz) creamed coconut blended with
    250 ml (8 fl oz) boiling water

1 large mango, halved and stone removed

142 ml (5 fl oz) soured cream

2 tablespoons chopped fresh coriander

salt

❶ Heat the oil in a heavy-based pan and fry the chicken until sealed all over. Remove from the pan.

❷ Add the onion to the pan and fry gently until softened. Add the garlic and spices and stir-fry for 1 minute more.

❸ Add the coconut liquid and the chicken to the pan with salt to taste. Cover and simmer gently for 10 minutes.

❹ Meanwhile, peel the mango and cut in slices. Add to the pan with the soured cream and coriander and simmer for a few minutes until heated through. Serve with Basmati rice and mango chutney.

Chicken with Cous Cous and Fresh Dates

Preparation and cooking time: 45 minutes.
Freezing: not recommended. Serves 4.

Cous cous is a speciality in Tunisia, Algeria and Morocco and is made from pre-cooked semolina grain. Cous cous recipes usually include a meat or sausage, some sort of dried fruit such as dates, apricots or raisins, as well as vegetables.

3 tablespoons olive oil + 2 teaspoons for the
   cous cous
2 onions, sliced
8 small skinless chicken thighs
2 garlic cloves, chopped
½ teaspoon saffron powder
1 teaspoon paprika
2 teaspoons ground cinnamon
1 small chilli pepper, de-seeded and chopped
600 ml (1 pint) chicken stock
1 parsnip, cut in chunks

3 carrots, sliced
250 g (8 oz) broad beans
400 g (13 oz) can of chopped tomatoes
420 g can of chick peas, drained
4 courgettes, sliced
75 g (3 oz) fresh dates, halved and stoned
75 g (3 oz) ready-to-eat dried apricots,
   chopped
300 g (10 oz) cous cous
1 teaspoon salt + extra for seasoning
600 ml (1 pint) boiling water

❶ Heat the 3 tablespoons of oil in a large, heavy-based pan and fry the onions and chicken thighs briskly, stirring occasionally, until they begin to brown.

❷ Add the garlic, spices, chilli pepper, stock and salt to taste, and then stir in the parsnip, carrots, broad beans, tomatoes and chick peas. Bring to a boil, cover and simmer gently for 20 minutes.

❸ Add the courgettes, dates and apricots, cover and cook for 10 minutes more.

❹ Meanwhile, put the cous cous in a bowl with 1 teaspoon of salt and pour the boiling water over the top. Leave to soak for 5 minutes and then add the 2 teaspoons of oil and mix with a fork to fluff it up.

❺ Pile the cous cous in a mound on a large shallow serving platter. Use a slotted spoon to lift the chicken and vegetables from the pan. Make a depression on top of the cous cous, spoon on a little of the sauce and serve the rest separately.

Chicken Biryani

Preparation and cooking time: 45 minutes.
Freezing: not recommended. Serves 4.

Biryani is a festive Indian dish of Mogul origin and it is important to use Basmati rice to achieve the right flavour. Saffron is used to give it an authentic fragrance and it should be streaked with yellow. This is a simplified version but is, nevertheless, delicious.

4 tablespoons sunflower oil

4 cardamom pods, seeds removed and
   crushed

1 teaspoon cumin seeds

6 cloves

2.5 cm (1-inch) piece of fresh root ginger,
   chopped finely

2 garlic cloves, crushed

500 g (1 lb) breast of chicken, cut in cubes

1 teaspoon ground cinnamon

½ teaspoon chilli powder

150 g (5 oz) yogurt

150 ml (¼ pint) chicken stock

1 teaspoon salt

350 g (12 oz) Basmati rice

1½ teaspoons saffron threads in 3
   tablespoons boiling water

2 onions, sliced finely

25 g (1 oz) slivered almonds

25 g (1 oz) sultanas

❶ Preheat the oven to Gas Mark 5/ 190°C/375°F.

❷ Heat 2 tablespoons of the oil in a heavy-based pan. Add the cardamom seeds, cumin seeds, cloves, ginger, garlic and chicken and stir-fry for 3 minutes, until the chicken is sealed.

❸ Add the cinnamon and chilli powder and fry for 1 minute. Stir in the yogurt a little at a time, stirring well between each addition. Add the stock and salt. Cover and cook for 10 minutes.

❹ Meanwhile, cook the rice in a large pan of boiling salted water for 6 minutes. Drain thoroughly.

❺ Place the chicken in the bottom of a casserole dish. Cover with the rice and sprinkle with the saffron water. Cover and cook in the oven for 25 minutes until the rice is tender.

❻ Meanwhile, heat the remaining oil in a frying pan and fry the onions until golden brown and crisp. Remove from the pan and keep warm. Add the almonds to the pan and fry until golden, and then add the sultanas and fry briefly until they plump up.

❼ Transfer the chicken and rice to a heated serving platter. Sprinkle with the fried onions, almonds and sultanas and serve with a cucumber or banana raita.

Chinese Chicken Wings

Preparation and cooking time: 25 minutes.
Freezing: not recommended. Serves 4.

These make a good starter but are very sticky – provide plenty of napkins!

2 tablespoons clear honey

1 tablespoon tomato ketchup

1 tablespoon soy sauce

1 garlic clove, crushed

½ teaspoon five-spice powder

½ teaspoon chilli powder

8 chicken wings, cut in half with tips removed

For the fried 'seaweed':

250 g (8 oz) spring greens, shredded finely

oil for deep-frying

salt

caster sugar

❶ Preheat the oven to Gas Mark 7/ 220°C/425°F.

❷ Mix together the honey, ketchup, soy sauce, garlic, five-spice and chilli powders and brush liberally over the chicken pieces to coat completely.

❸ Put the wings in a baking tin and cook for 20 minutes, turning once and basting with lots more of the sauce.

❹ For the 'seaweed', deep-fry the spring greens in hot oil in batches. Drain well on kitchen paper. Sprinkle with salt and caster sugar to taste and serve with the chicken wings.

Chinese Chicken and Sesame Salad

Preparation and cooking time: 15 minutes.
Freezing: not recommended. Serves 4.

Sesame oil and soy give this salad its Eastern flavour.

250 g (8 oz) cooked chicken breast, cut in strips

1 red pepper, halved, de-seeded and cut in strips

175 g (6 oz) mange-tout, cut in half on the diagonal

227 g can of water chestnuts, drained and sliced

175 g (6 oz) button mushrooms, sliced

1 bunch watercress

1 tablespoon sesame seeds

For the dressing:

2 tablespoons sesame paste

1 teaspoon sesame oil

1 garlic clove, crushed

1 teaspoon dark soy sauce

2 tablespoons cider vinegar

2 tablespoons dry sherry

1 teaspoon clear honey

❶ Place the chicken strips in a bowl with the red pepper, mange-tout, chestnuts and mushrooms.

❷ Blend the sesame paste with the oil, garlic and soy sauce until smooth. Whisk in the vinegar, sherry and honey.

❸ Pour over the chicken mixture and toss thoroughly.

❹ Arrange the watercress on a serving plate and pile the salad in the middle. Sprinkle the sesame seeds over the top and serve at once.

Catalan Chicken Casserole

Preparation and cooking time: 40 minutes.
Freezing: recommended. Serves 4.

This robust peasant dish from northern Spain incorporates all the flavours of the Mediterranean.

2 tablespoons olive oil
4 chicken joints
1 large onion, sliced
1 red pepper, de-seeded and sliced
2 garlic cloves, sliced
1 tablespoon paprika
1 tablespoon flour
400 g (13 oz) can of chopped tomatoes

300 ml (½ pint) chicken stock
½ teaspoon sugar
150 ml (¼ pint) white wine
1 tablespoon tomato purée
75 g (3 oz) chorizo sausage, sliced
25 g (1 oz) black olives, halved and stoned
2 tablespoons chopped fresh parsley
salt and freshly ground black pepper

❶ Heat the oil in a heavy-based flameproof casserole, fry the chicken joints on all sides until golden brown, and then remove from the pan.

❷ Add the onion, red pepper and garlic and cook for 5 minutes, until softened. Stir in the paprika and flour.

❸ Add the tomatoes, stock, sugar, wine and tomato purée and bring to a boil. Return the chicken joints to the pan, cover and simmer gently for 25–30 minutes until the chicken is cooked.

❹ Stir in the chorizo sausage, black olives, parsley and seasoning to taste and heat through. Serve with boiled potatoes.

Nasi Goreng

Preparation and cooking time: 30 minutes.
Freezing: not recommended. Serves 4.

This Indonesian speciality of spiced rice with chicken and prawns is served with thin strips of omelette sprinkled over the top.

2 tablespoons sunflower oil

2 onions, sliced

250 g (8 oz) chicken breast, cut in cubes

2 garlic cloves, sliced

1 red chilli, de-seeded and sliced thinly

250 g (8 oz) long-grain rice, cooked

125 g (4 oz) prawns

1 tablespoon light soy sauce

1 egg

$\frac{1}{4}$ teaspoon chilli powder

2 spring onions, chopped finely

1 tablespoon chopped fresh coriander

salt and freshly ground black pepper

cucumber slices, to garnish

For the mango sambal:

1 small mango

1 small onion, chopped

2 tablespoons chopped fresh coriander

1 small green chilli, de-seeded and chopped

juice of 1 lime

❶ Heat the oil in a wok or heavy-based pan and fry the onions and chicken for 4–5 minutes, until the chicken is cooked and the onion softened.

❷ Add the garlic and chilli and fry for 1 minute, and then stir in the rice, prawns, soy sauce and seasoning to taste.

❸ Stir-fry for 4–5 minutes until it is all heated through. Transfer to a warm serving dish, cover and keep warm.

❹ Put the egg in a bowl and whisk together with the chilli powder, spring onions and salt to taste.

❺ Pour into a 20 cm (8-inch) heated omelette pan and cook gently until set. Remove from the pan, cool and shred finely.

❻ Arrange the omelette over the rice, sprinkle with the chopped coriander, garnish with cucumber slices and serve with mango sambal.

❻ For the mango sambal peel and stone the mango. Chop the flesh and put in a bowl with the onion, the chopped fresh coriander, the chilli and the lime juice. Mix together thoroughly.

Chicken and Prune Tagine

Preparation and cooking time: 40 minutes.
Freezing: recommended. Serves 4.

This Moroccan speciality is traditionally served in a large earthenware dish with a domed lid called a *tagine*, but any covered casserole dish will do. Moroccans include spices and fruit of all types with their casseroles – dates, prunes, apricots and raisins are the most commonly used.

3 tablespoons olive oil

500 g (1 lb) skinless chicken breast, cut in
   large pieces

2 onions, cut in wedges

1 red pepper, de-seeded and cut in large
   pieces

1 teaspoon ground cinnamon

1 teaspoon ground ginger

½ teaspoon chilli powder

1 tablespoon flour

450 ml (¾ pint) hot stock

250 g (8 oz) pitted prunes

15 g (½ oz) butter

25 g (1 oz) slivered almonds

salt and freshly ground black pepper

❶ Heat the oil in a casserole and fry the chicken until sealed all over. Remove from the pan.

❷ Add the onions and pepper and fry, stirring frequently, until it begins to brown. Add the spices and flour and cook for 1 minute more.

❸ Add the stock, prunes and seasoning to taste and bring to a boil. Return the chicken to the casserole, cover and simmer gently for 30 minutes.

❹ Meanwhile, heat the butter in a small pan and fry the almonds until pale golden brown.

❺ Sprinkle over the tagine and serve with cous cous or boiled rice.

Teriyaki Chicken with Fried Cabbage

Preparation and cooking time: 15 minutes.
Freezing: not recommended. Serves 4.

This tasty dish is made with succulent chicken strips in a soy and sesame marinade which is then used to flavour the fried cabbage.

3 tablespoons soy sauce

2 tablespoons sherry

2 garlic cloves, crushed

2.5 cm (1-inch) piece fresh root ginger, chopped finely

1 tablespoon sesame oil

350 g (12 oz) skinless chicken fillet, cut in strips

2 tablespoons groundnut oil

1 red pepper, de-seeded and cut in strips

750 g (1½ lb) savoy cabbage, shredded finely

❶ Mix together the soy sauce, sherry, garlic, ginger and sesame oil in a shallow dish. Stir in the chicken strips until thoroughly coated.

❷ Weave the chicken strips on to satay sticks to resemble snakes. Grill for 5–6 minutes until cooked, turning them once.

❸ Meanwhile, heat the groundnut oil in a wok, add the red pepper and cabbage and stir-fry for 2 minutes.

❹ Add the remaining marinade and stir-fry for 3 minutes more.

❺ Arrange 2 satay sticks on each plate and serve with the cabbage.

Index